# Neither Here Nor There

## THE ART OF

## *Oliver Jeffers*

gestalten

**Neither Here Nor There**
**The Art of Oliver Jeffers**

Edited by Richard Seabrooke
Foreword by Richard Seabrooke
Introduction by Mac Premo

Cover by Oliver Jeffers
Layout by Conor & David
Typeface: Monotype Grotesque by
Frank Hinman Pierpont for Monotype, 1926

Project management by Elisabeth Honerla for Gestalten
Production management by Janine Milstrey for Gestalten
Proofreading by Devin Gordon and Charlotte Barker

In collaboration with  The Small Print
www.thesmallprint.ie

Printed by Graphicom srl, Vicenza
Made in Europe

Published by Gestalten, Berlin 2012
**ISBN 978-3-89955-447-2**

For more information, please visit www.gestalten.com.

Bibliographic information published by the Deutsche
Nationalbibliothek. The Deutsche Nationalbibliothek lists
this publication in the Deutsche Nationalbibliografie; detailed
bibliographic data are available online at http://dnb.d-nb.de.

This book was printed according to the internationally accepted
ISO 14001 standards for environmental protection, which specify
requirements for an environmental management system.

This book was printed on paper certified by the FSC®.

Gestalten is a climate-neutral company. We collaborate with the
non-profit carbon offset provider myclimate (www.myclimate.org)
to neutralize the company's carbon footprint produced through
our worldwide business activities by investing in projects that
reduce $CO_2$ emissions (www.gestalten.com/myclimate).

Protect our planet

*Cover*
**Replacing Adrianna in**
**Three Parts (detail)**
by Oliver Jeffers

⊢ : Hp . ⊃ . μ +c 1 = ξ̂ {(∃y) . y ⊂ sm "μ . y ε ξ . ξ −ι'y}

[*13.195] = ξ̂ {(∃y) . y ε ξ . ξ −ι'y ⊂ sm "μ} : ⊢ . Prop

*110·64 ⊢ . 0 +c 0 = 0 [*110·62]

*110·641 ⊢ . 1 +c 0 = 0 +c 1 = 1 [*110·51 . 11 . *101·2]

*110·642 ⊢ . 2 +c 0 = 0 +c 2 = 2 [*110·51 . 11 . *101·31]

*110·643 ⊢ . 1 +c 1 = 2

Dem.

⊢ . *110·632 . *101·2 . (8 . )
⊢ . 1 +c 1 = ξ̂ {(∃y) . y ε ξ . ξ −y

[*54·3] = 2 . ) ⊢ . Prop

THE ABOVE PROPOSITION IS OCCASIONALLY USEF
AT LEAST THREE TIMES IN *113·66
AND *120· 123·472

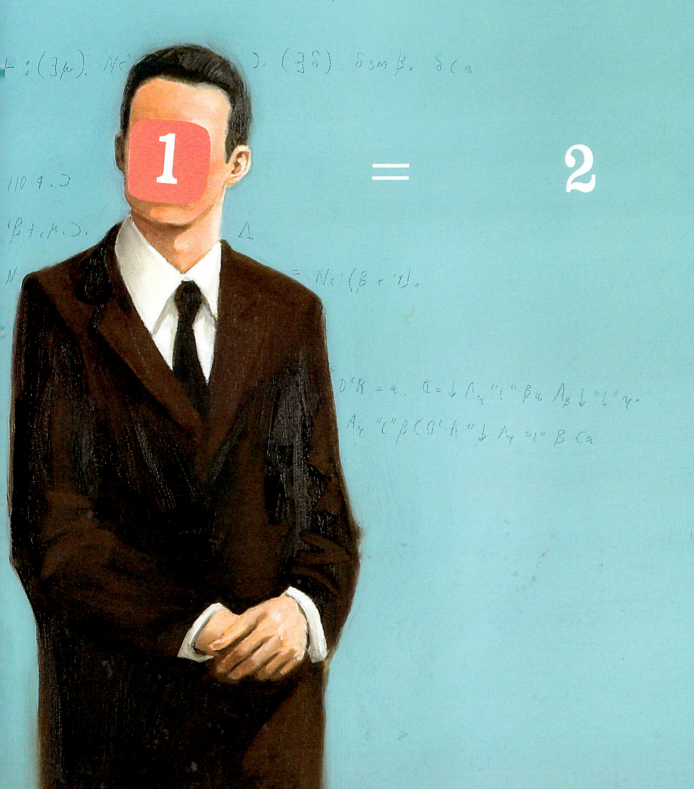

**Russell and Whitehead**

2006

oil and vinyl on canvas

80cm × 120cm

**I Don't Care**

2006

acrylic and letraset on old book cover

50cm × 50cm

Oliver is a curious guy.

He's curious about nearly everything around him. Mathematics and science, friendships and family ties, nostalgia and modernity, popular culture and legend, humour and seriousness, antiques and shiny new stuff, the tiniest of things, the largest of things, food, drink, household tools, even the odd moose and penguin—all find a home in Oliver's brain and a place in his notebooks.

He's especially curious about the idea of duality. The concept that something can mean one thing to one person, and something entirely different to another. And he likes thinking about the ways that society attempts to bridge the divide by creating systems of logic: mathematical equations, Pantone colour matching systems, units of measure for charting the depths of the sea...

One of the things that excites Oliver about duality is that it always eventually leads to an unanswerable, unresolvable scenario. It's an attempt to apply logic and reason to the emotional and irrational, forcing the left brain and the right brain to work together, only to find that one can't really explain the other. It's this blending—the emotiveness of painting and the clinical rigor of mathematics, and the way in which they represent opposing systems by which we try to understand our world—that Oliver explores in his art.

Born in Australia, Oliver spent his childhood and young adulthood in Belfast, Northern Ireland, but now calls Brooklyn, NY home. He has explored the world many times over, and for me, it's this hunger for influences and experiences, both old and new, that defines Oliver and his work.

He's a collector of ideas and ephemera that, at some point, maybe years down the line, maybe that very afternoon, will play their part in his latest creation. He's willing to make a mistake, although I'm not sure he ever does, really. As an artist, he is as comfortable flying solo as leading the charge, working with others on whatever crosses his doorstep and sparks his imagination. All while dreaming of home, fresh Veda bread, good aged whiskey, and a solid chat.

His work ethic is also quite curious. Where others wait for inspiration, Oliver demands it of himself every day, and he works diligently to make sure every piece shines. If you visit his studio, you will find many started pieces awaiting that final killer idea to transform them into something he can stamp as done. Some pieces just take a little longer as he moves stuff around. Some are awaiting a chance encounter that causes an idea to alight in his brain, some just require the time for him to access the vast creative archive housed deep in his subconscious.

He always gets there, or at least I think he does. (He's not saying otherwise.) Much like Oliver's life, though, it's the journey of creation that proves as rewarding and enjoyable as the ultimate destination.

**Richard Seabrooke**
*The Small Print*

"Man is unique not because he does science, and he is unique not because he does art, but because science and art equally are expressions of his marvelous plasticity of mind."
—Jacob Bronowski

"Dualities occur all over the place."
—Oliver Jeffers

After multiple conversations with a Doctor of Quantum Physics, Jeffers half jokingly made this piece as a commentary on the possible dangers of over-analyzing something to the point of it being unrecognizable. The Pantone reference numbers were placed on as additional information, irrelevant to the need of an individual looking to appreciate the color palatte used. The 'Homage to Ferdinand Bauer' is a nod to a natural history artist in the 18th century who developed and memorized a color chart that contained over 1,000 colors.

Gilding the Lily
(An Homage to Ferdinand Bauer)
2006
oil and letraset on canvas in gilded frame
93cm × 77cm

Oliver Jeffer's work is almost always about only two things. Those two things, however, constantly change. They don't compete for dominance—rather, they jockey for position in contextual relevance. Fittingly, here's how he once answered a question from an interviewer about whether he believes in an objective reality:

"I don't know how to answer that. Sometimes I do. Sometimes I don't."

When Oliver was a child, his father—perhaps his greatest influence—would often remind him: "Your version of the truth is not the same as somebody else's." It's a statement that champions tolerance, a kind of ethical pragmatism.

In scientific terms, it's the uncertainty principle, which states that the more precisely one property is measured, the more difficult it becomes to measure the other. Therein lies the challenge that fascinates Oliver: "I'm trying to take one thing and see if it can be looked at from both the emotional and the logical point of view, exactly at the same time." According to Oliver, this seeming paradox represents two very important facets of existence, fairness and the pursuit of truth.

What gives Oliver's work its animating life is another oft-repeated line by his father: "Never let the truth get in the way of a good story."

While Oliver is deeply concerned with the balance of cold science and warm emotion, he adjusts the temperature of his viewers' experience with an engaging and gregarious palette. You are invited into his paintings, you'll be in good company, and only asked to share the wonderment of the question they pose or answer they suggest, never to prove yourself worthy of some demanded contemplation.

**11**

**Book (Week 11)**
2004
mixed media
28cm × 44cm

**One of Two Giants**
2004
oil on canvas
160cm × 210cm

In much of his work, Oliver attempts to reconcile the philosophical impasse at which art and science often find themselves. One is by nature subjective, while the other is defined by the pursuit of objectivity. Ultimately, each seeks to explain or at least address the condition of our existence.

In 2002, Oliver and I—who have been friends since our childhood—worked together on a project called *Book*. For 36 weeks, a sketchbook was passed back and forth between four artists: Oliver and his brother Rory in Belfast, and two based in Brooklyn, NY—myself and our friend Duke Riley. Each of us had five days to respond to the work on the pages that preceded his own. We did not say a word to each other about the individual spreads until the completion of the project; only then did we sit down and discuss the intended meanings of each spread and their subsequent interpretation by the next artist in line. Oliver's first formal investigation into the idea of duality happened during the making of *Book*. It was Week 11: we see the portrait of a man reading a paper. In front of him are two glasses, one filled with orange juice, the other with milk. We have all experienced that moment when we expect one specific taste but experience a different one—the shock of a defied sensory expectation. It's strange and uncomfortable and uniquely disorienting.

Consider another piece of Oliver's: *Understanding Everything*, in which we see another glass of juice on a table. To the right of the glass is the complex shadow / reflection that happens when light is cast through glass. Immediately to the glass's left, in the direction from which the light is coming, is a complex mathematical equation. This equation represents the refraction of light.

Another aspect of Oliver's art is the idea of creating and hiding. The theory championed by quantum physicist Erwin Schrödinger suggests that the process of observation affects the thing being observed. But what if something is hidden? To examine this, Oliver has begun completing paintings and then obscuring them by dipping them in paint or covering them with fogged glass. If meaning is conveyed visually, what happens to meaning when the visual is obscured? The act of hiding a finished painting yanks a completed form back into an incomplete state.

But the key, fundamental duality explored in Oliver's work is his ability to package daunting questions in accessible form. His work is unique, engaging, and inviting, and yet somehow also reassuringly familiar. But just past that welcome mat are questions that have been dogging humanity for millennia. When asked if he expects to figure it all out, Oliver has just the right answer:

"Um. I think I will, and I won't."

**Mac Premo**

Two stories about giants play out in this composition set in contemporary Belfast, Northern Ireland. Firstly, the biblical tale of David and Goliath (Goliath is also the name of the crane pictured) depicts the underdog defeating the terrible foe against all odds; good overcoming evil in a dramatic and heroic battle. The second and more significant giant reference is to Cervantes's 'Don Quixote,' in which insanity is a major theme.

ere

**Seagulls Will Inherit the Earth**

2004

oil and chalk on canvas

100cm × 130cm

**The Process of Running Away**

2004

oil on canvas

50cm × 70cm

**I Can Shout Louder**

2004

oil and chalk on canvas

40cm × 60cm

**12 12**

2005

mixed media

42cm × 30cm

**Ocean Man**
2005
oil on canvas
40cm × 90cm

**Concentrate**

2004

acrylic on canvas

30cm × 30cm

**Broken**

2004

oil, chalk, and letraset on canvas

50cm × 50cm

**How Much Does Your Voice Weigh?**

2004

oil, pencil, and letraset on canvas

40cm × 60cm

**The End of Modernism**
2006
oil on canvas
60cm × 90cm

**Selfish**

2004

acrylic, screenprint, and chalk on canvas

70cm × 110cm

**Soap**
2004
acrylic, chalk, and letraset on canvas
70cm × 130cm

01.

**Music (Part 1)**

2004

acrylic on canvas

70cm × 100cm

**Music (Part 2)**
2004
acrylic on canvas
70cm × 100cm

Painted at the time when global warming had just entered the main public vocabulary, 'Assessing the Danger' uses the visual lexicon of maritime warning systems as an analogy for the old adage 'There are none as blind as those who don't want to see.' The multiple lighthouses suggest an impending doom just over the horizon, the significance of which is betrayed by the calmness of the scene.

**Assessing the Danger**

2006

oil on canvas

100cm × 160cm

**The Bigger Picture (Part 1)**
2006
oil on canvas
60cm × 90cm

—»
**The Bigger Picture (Part 2)**
2006
oil and letraset on canvas
60cm × 90cm

In these paintings, Jeffers considers basic
human curiosity, its seeming insignificance
amid the vastness of the environment in
which our planet sits, and the subsequent
futility of human endeavors to understand
this space. It was not a period of optimism
for the artist.

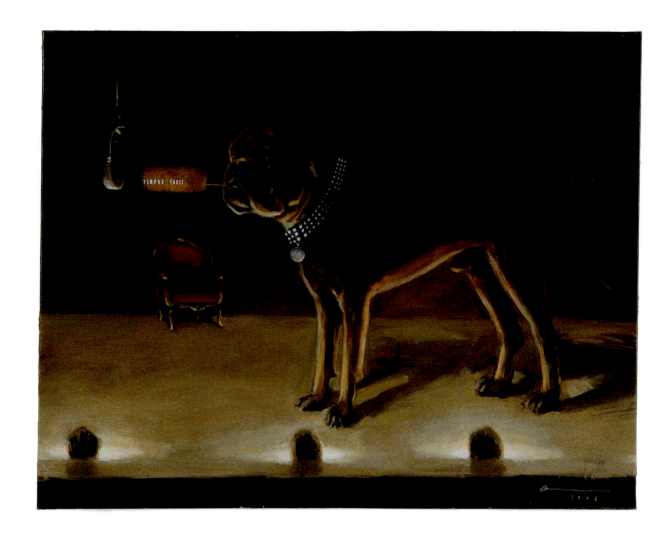

**Ollie**

2006

oil on canvas

120cm × 155cm

**This is Not a Place**

2004

oil and chalk on canvas

30cm × 42cm

**Suspended**
2006
oil on canvas
140cm × 52cm

—»
**The Depiction of Beauty**
2006
oil and vinyl on canvas
160cm × 100cm

$$\frac{1}{8}\left(\frac{9}{\mu^2} - 1\right)^2$$

**Understanding Everything**

*2004*

oil and letraset on canvas

100cm × 60cm

After a long period of exploring the relationship between words and images in his compositions, this painting is a first comparison between the emotive nature of painting and the clinical nature of mathematics, and how they both represent opposing systems by which we try to understand our world. The equation refers to how light refracts through glass and is positioned to serve as the source of light that illuminates the table.

RED FISH IN WINTER

**Red Fish in Winter**
2005
oil on canvas
50cm × 65cm

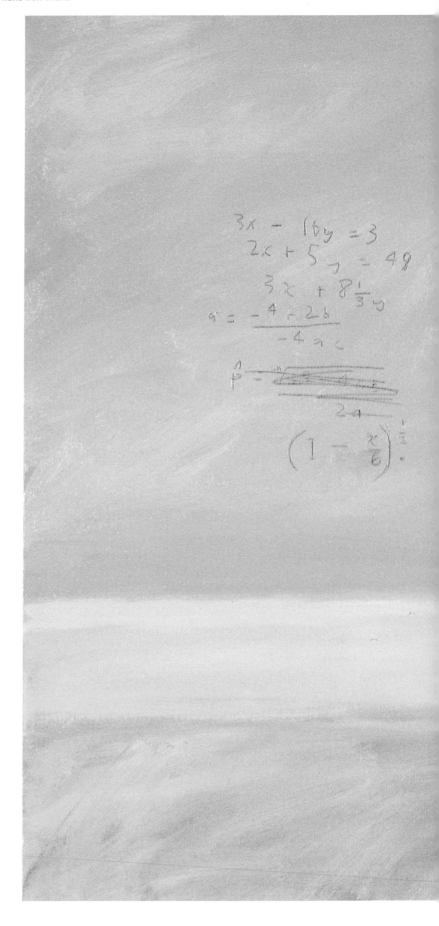

**Still Life with Maths and Orange**

2006

oil, letraset, and lead on canvas

60cm × 90cm

**Imagine You are Running**

2006

oil, letraset, and charcoal on canvas

40cm × 60cm

**Gillespie's Thoughts Were Elsewhere**

2006

oil on canvas

60cm × 90cm

—»

**The Substitute Window**

2004

oil on canvas

100cm × 160cm

The house painted in the sparse landscape is the building where Jeffers grew up, removed from the street on which it usually sits. The title comes from an imaginary window in a solid wall in another building where the artist lived, and the composition is the imaginary view he would see if there was one there. It serves as a means of paying tribute to his past amid a continually nomadic lifestyle.

47

$$\frac{1}{8}\left(\frac{9}{\mu^2} - 1\right)$$

**Still Life with Logic
and a Choice of Beverage**
2006
oil and letraset on canvas
70cm × 90cm

$$f_{\text{atmos}} = \left[ 1 + \frac{(\text{PCO}_2)_0}{\text{PCO}_2} [\text{CO}_3{}^{2-}]_0 \frac{V}{M_0} \right]^{-1}$$

«—

**Incompleteness: Knowing
More than You Can Tell**

2006

oil and vinyl on canvas

120cm × 80cm

**Population of the World at Last Count**

2006

oil and vinyl on canvas

100cm × 160cm

**Landscape with Trajectory and Metal**

2006

oil and vinyl on linen

77cm × 122cm

In order for the equation of trajectory to be satisfied, the car must pass through the point (x1, y1), at a speed of *u* and at an angle *x* to a horizontal plane. This is a scene of extreme emotional significance analyzed through the lens of clinical mathematical logic.

The equation shown in the painting:

$$gx_1^2 \tan^2 \alpha - 2u^2 x_1 \tan \alpha + 2u^2 y_1 + gx_1^2 = 0.$$

$P(x_1, y_1)$

$$x \oplus y = x + y,$$
$$\text{if } x, y < 57$$
$$= 5 \text{ otherwise}$$

**Not a Something,**
**But Not a Nothing Either**
2006
oil and vinyl on canvas
120cm × 80cm

$$v_i = \pi_i - \alpha_i \left( \left| \pi_i^f - \pi_i \right| - \sum_{j \neq i}^{n} \beta_i \left| \pi_j^f - \pi_i \right| \right).$$

**Portrait with a Notion of Victory**

2006

oil and vinyl on canvas

121cm × 81cm

57

NEITHER HERE NOR THERE

$$z \longrightarrow z^2 + c$$

**Still Life with Control and Chaos**
2007
oil and vinyl on canvas
28cm × 51cm

$$\lambda = {}^{h}/_{mv}$$

**Still Life with Light and Lightbulb**

2007

oil and vinyl on canvas

35cm × 46cm

—»

**What It's Like**

2006

oil, letraset, resin, canvas, and wood

77cm × 61cm

Jeffers's various exercises in exploring the same subject matter through two different lenses (art and science), are no better illustrated than in this painting. The equation, which is often cited as depicting the connection between the wave and the particle nature of light, does exactly that. Here Jeffers looks closely at the notion that we can define something by how we choose to look at it.

$$\psi = \sum_k c_k |\psi_k\rangle \longrightarrow |\psi_j\rangle.$$

A.

The Weight of the World

2006

oil and vinyl on canvas

100cm × 70cm

Vaderology

2007

car paint, varnish, pencil, and letraset

on replica Darth Vader helmet

**Denis**

2007

oil on canvas

130cm × 100cm

**Walter**

2007

oil on canvas

130cm × 100cm

«—

**Sam**

2007

oil on canvas

130cm × 100cm

**Michael & Marco**

2007

oil on canvas

130cm × 100cm

**Look the Other Way**

2006

googley eyes on salvaged photograph

30cm × 44cm

**Song Writing Machine**

2006

typewriter, guitar neck, and glue

42cm × 30cm × 20cm

'e

here

# Book

«—
**Book**
2004
mixed media
28cm × 44cm

In 2002 Oliver collaborated with New York-based artists Mac Premo and Duke Riley, as well as Oliver's long time work partner, his older brother Rory, on *Book*. Over the course of nine months, the four artists exchanged a standard black hardback sketchbook between them in random order. By its completion, *Book* had travelled over 60,000 miles between Belfast and New York. Before sending it to the next participant, each artist had only five days to complete a double-page spread in response to the one that preceded it.

Other than this, there was no communication between the four concerning the content of *Book* during its making. As a side effect, the predominant theme of the project was not about how things are interpreted so much as the role misinterpretation plays in shaping the course of conversation. *Book* was exhibited in both Belfast and New York.

In 2008, five years on, all four artists agreed to do the project again. After a few weeks, the strict deadline of five days to complete a spread was dropped due to the artists' very different lifestyles and work schedules this time around. As of going to print for this publication, four years later, *Book 2* is still ongoing.

squeak

**Book (Week 16)**

2004

mixed media

28cm × 44cm

—»

*(clockwise from top left)*

**Weeks 21, 5, 2, and 8**

*Spreads from*
**Book 2**
2011
mixed media
28cm × 44cm

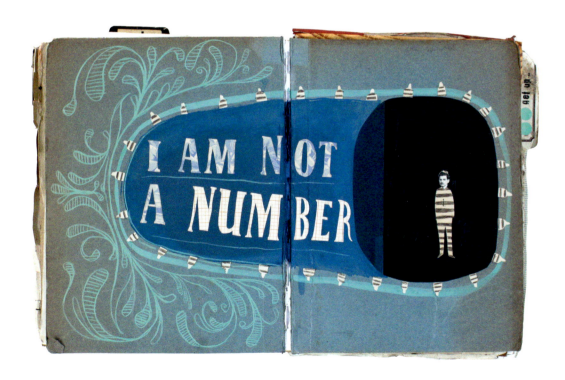

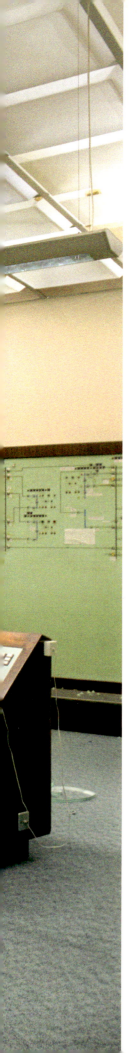

# Building

While completing the Belfast leg of the *Book* exhibition in 2004, the four artists were made aware of a derelict building that was earmarked for demolition. An ordinary 3-story brick-box building from the outside, the inside told a different story: for decades, the building was the electrical switch room for Greater Belfast—essentially a giant on/off switch for the city.

A building of that importance would have been an obvious target during the years of political unrest in Belfast commonly known as The Troubles. Subsequently, the building was decommissioned slowly over a long period of time, and by neglect. When a service the building provided became outmoded, the access to that machinery was simply restricted. They just closed the doors to that room. The result was a time capsule.

The artists immediately recognized the potential for another project, commissioned photographer Chris Heaney to document its current state, and managed to talk the building's new owners into letting them salvage as much of the old equipment as possible. The salvaged materials were used as the raw material for the artists to tell the building's story from four different perspectives: from inside; from outside; the people it affected; the job it was doing. The exhibition was site-specific, installed on the ground floor of the premises.

Oliver chose to explore the fact that no one knew it was there, that this building, arguably the most important in the city, was hidden in plain view. His grandmother worked directly across the street from it for a decade when it was fully functional and was completely unaware of its existence. He sought to recreate the moment of his discovery, and made small paintings about the equipment he found, organized it by function, and then hid it all in drawers of various desks, lockers, and cabinets (all of them also found within the building). The end experience was that anyone viewing the exhibition had to find or discover the work for themselves.

**Control Room**
2006
Photo by Christopher Heaney

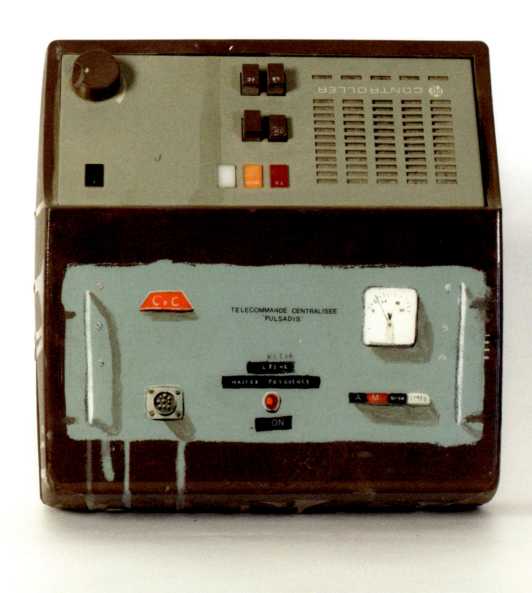

**Component of Measurement 6**

2006

mixed media

26cm × 10cm × 35cm

**Unplugged**

2006

mixed media

30cm × 45cm × 6cm

**Component of Measurement 8**

2006

mixed media

30cm × 26cm

—»

**Component of Measurement 1**

2006

mixed media

50cm × 30cm × 10cm

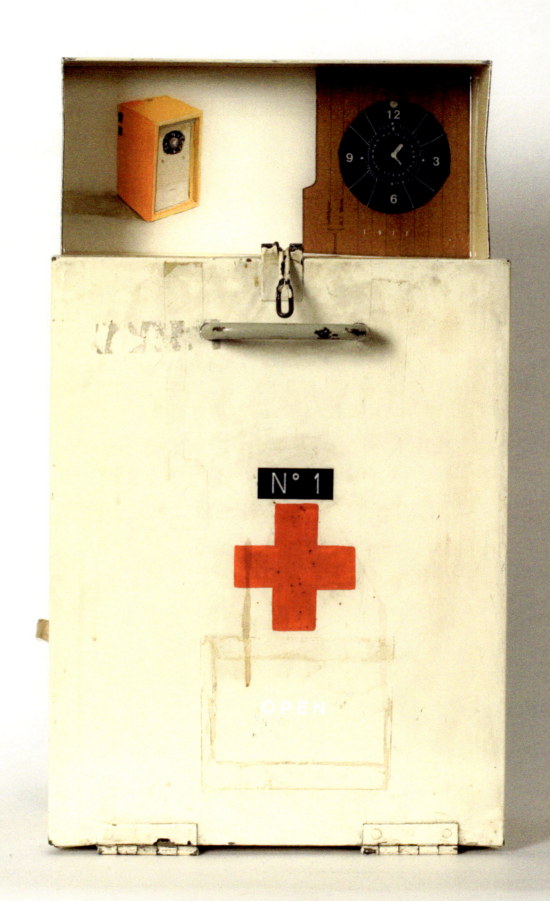

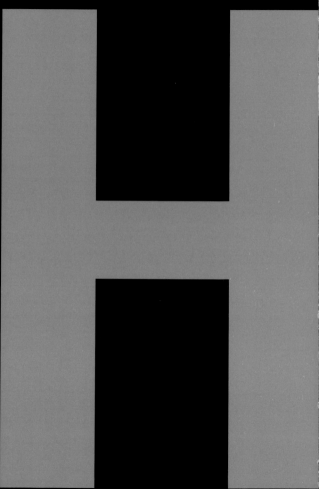

ere

**Still Life with Time No. 1**

2008

collage on wood

37cm × 57cm

**Still Life with Time Unplugged**

2011

oil on wood

24cm × 32cm

**Still Life with Time No. 2**

2009

oil on wood

20cm × 30cm

**The Witness**

2008

collage

10cm × 14cm

—»

**Still Life with Tea and Veda**

2008

collage

35cm × 30cm

Made in BELFAST →

STILL life with TEA and VEDA

**Before and After Painting No. 1**
2008
oil on canvas
60cm × 120cm

**Protracted Lanscape No. 2**

2009

oil and letraset on canvas

50cm × 60cm

Created in direct contrast to the Fathom Painting series, the numbers on this canvas serve to illustrate the angles of the earth at various points to the horizon – which is completely superfluous information. There is an irony at work that couples two flaws in human thinking; the distractions provided by over-analysis and the individual mind's ineffectual power when compared with the vast wealth of yet-undiscovered information.

94

**Short Story Machine**

2006

typewriter with altered keys

26cm × 31cm × 24cm

**Trouble**

2010

oil, letraset, collage,

and resin on wood

30cm × 30cm x 3cm

97

**Places in America**

2009

oil and chalk on wood

41cm × 70cm

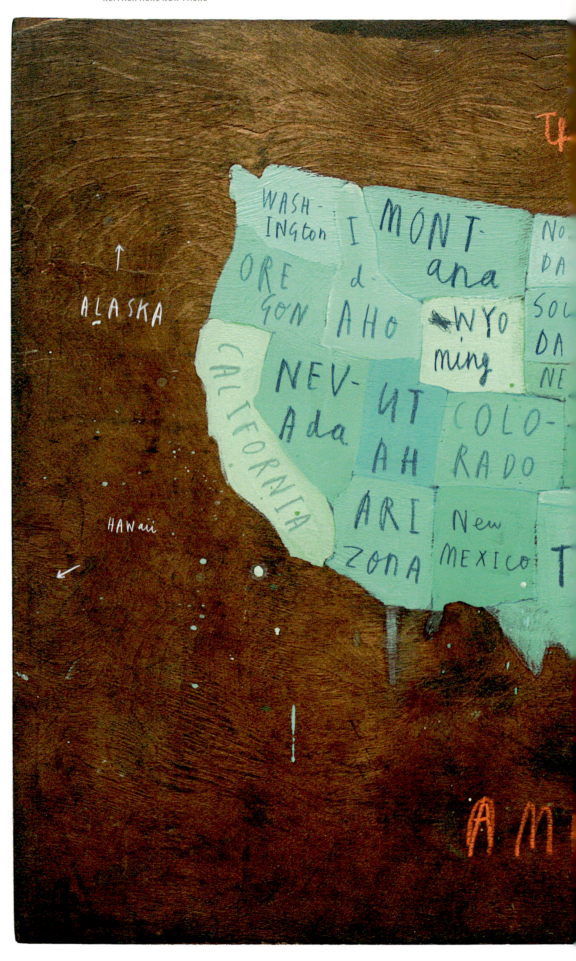

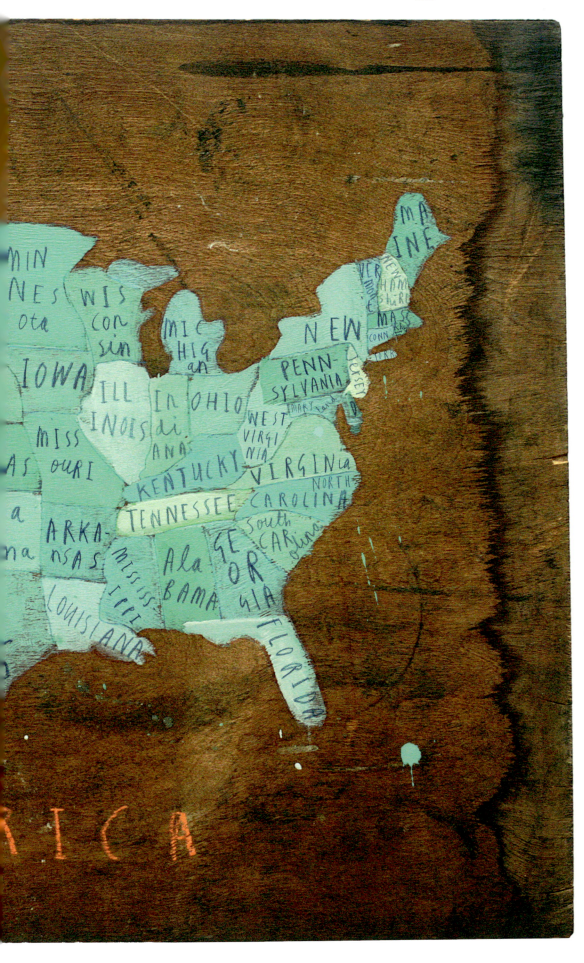

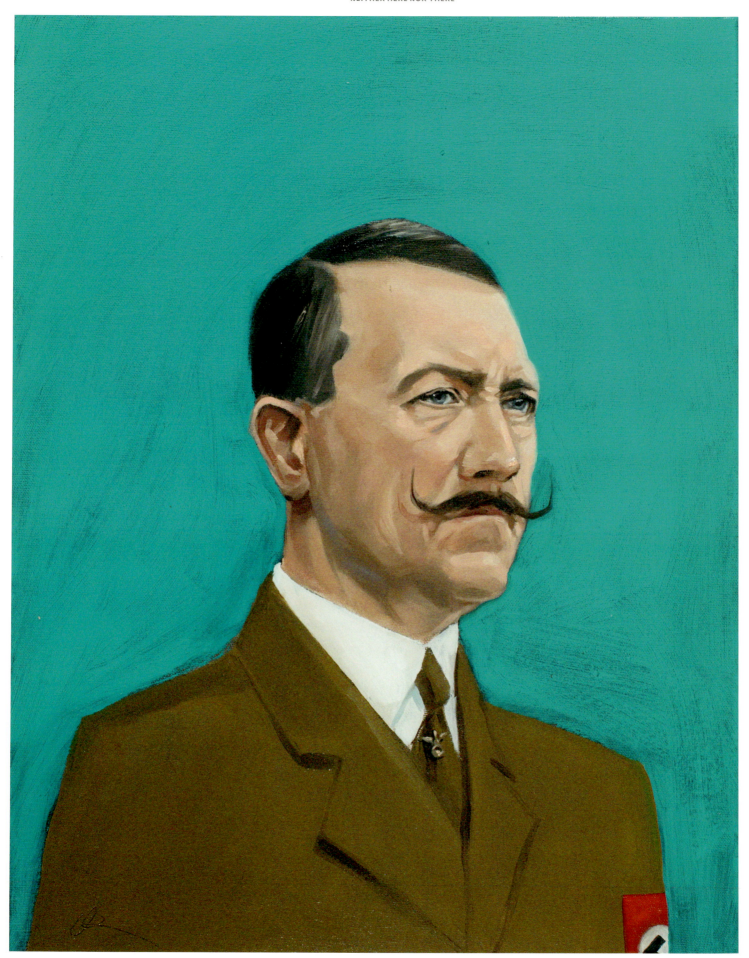

«—

**Adolf Dali**

2009

oil on canvas

51cm × 41cm

An alternative history that imagines a scenario in which Hitler had not been rejected from art school in Vienna, but instead continued his artistic career into adulthood.

**Ginger Hitler**

2012

oil on canvas

51cm × 41cm

**Maostache**

*Collaboration with Mac Premo*

2011

mixed media

44.5cm × 33cm

—»

**Uni Mao**

2012

mixed media

72cm × 52cm

伟大的领袖和导师毛泽东主席

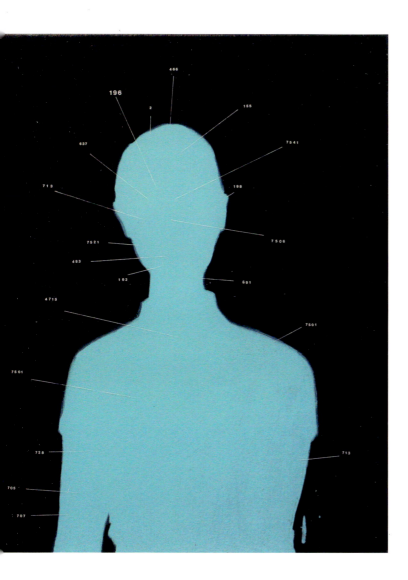

Further exploring the idea of examining the same subject matter from multiple perspectives, this triptych is one of the artist's earliest in the recurring theme of hidden information. The portrait on the left is slowly 'blue-screened' out as the viewer moves right, and the colors of paint and their locations are instead portrayed by Pantone numbers. In theory, this is all the information needed in order to be able to interpret the image.

**Replacing Adrianna in Three Parts**
2009
oil and letraset on canvas
60cm × 180cm (triptych)

7 5 2 7

*detail from*
**Replacing Adrianna in Three Parts**
2009

—»
**The Invisible Dog**
2011
oil on canvas
122cm × 91.5cm

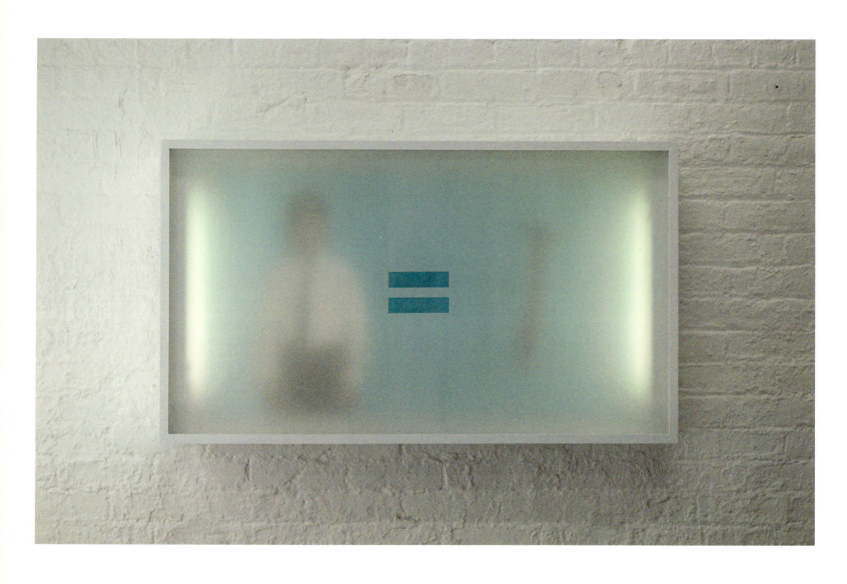

**Snowden's Secret (Part 1)**

2011

oil on painted canvas behind partially frosted glass

61cm × 107cm × 19cm

**Snowden's Secret (Part 2)**

2011

oil on painted canvas behind partially frosted glass

61cm × 107cm × 19cm

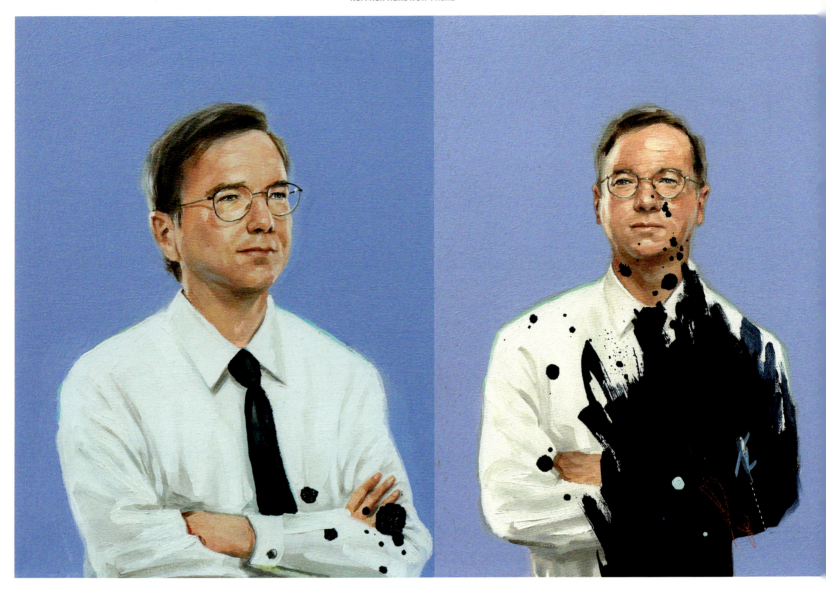

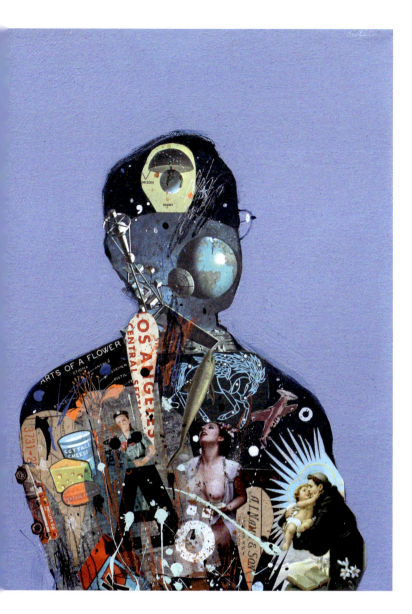

**The Search**

2008

oil and collage on canvas

34cm × 78cm (triptych)

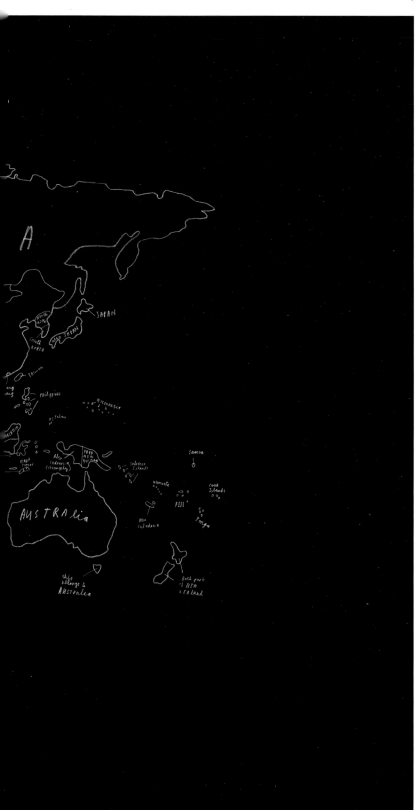

**Places on Earth**

2010

screenprint

66cm × 88cm

113

**Nothing is Forever Constant**
2012
oil on canvas
91cm × 122cm

**Fathom Painting No.1**

2010

oil and letraset on canvas

72cm × 122cm

The numbers on this canvas are fathoms, a now redundant system for measuring the depth of water. But as the surface of the ocean is forever changing, this painting explores the futility and pointlessness of measuring the immeasurable.

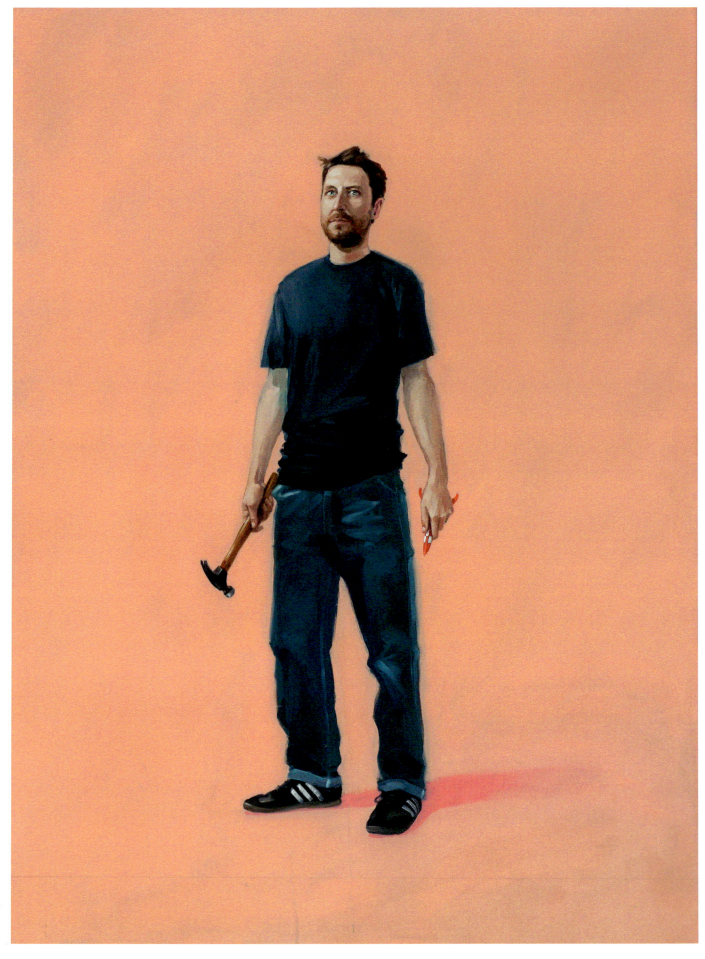

«—
**Making a Trade**
2010
oil on canvas
122cm × 92cm

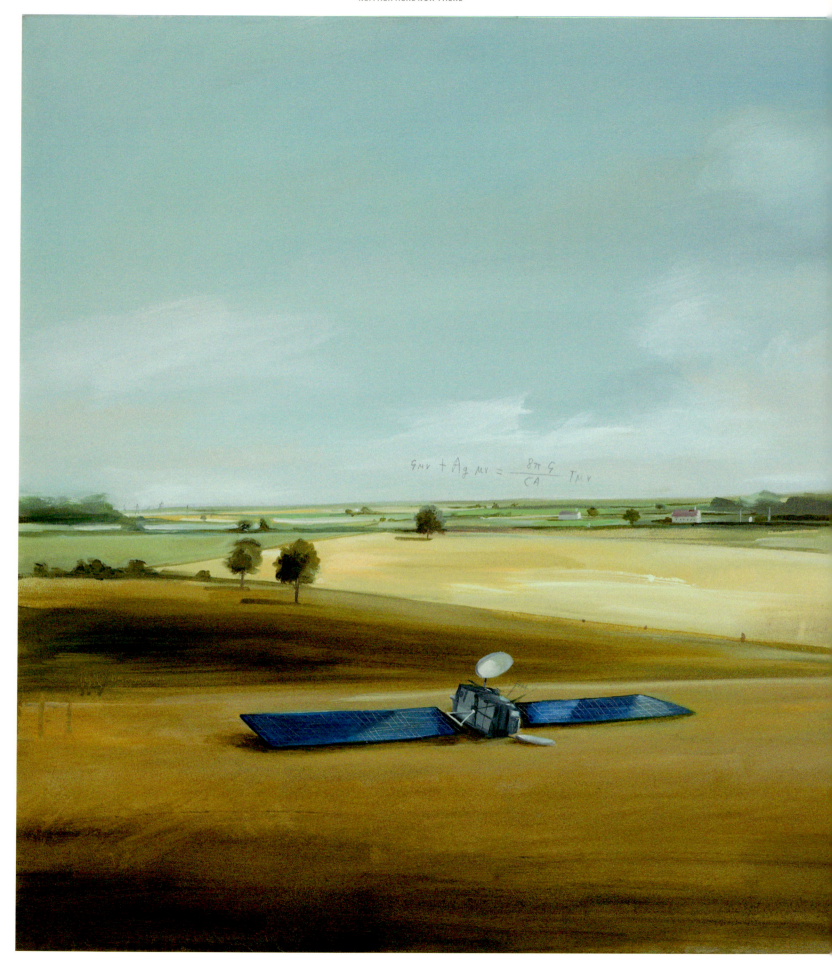

**Gravity**
2010
oil and graphite on canvas
72cm × 122cm

SHOOT TO KILL Son

Shoot to Kill
2011
collage
10.5cm × 15cm

—»
Dinner
2011
collage
29.7cm × 42cm

LETS  KILL  some  SHIT  for  DINNER

**Everywhere on Earth**

2011

oil on wood

163cm × 222cm

**Fathom Painting No. 2**
2012
oil on canvas
122cm × 91cm

**Seeing is Seeing (Part 2)**

2011

oil on canvas

86cm × 71cm

**I'm Going to Make My Dog Eat Glue**

2009

collage

10cm × 12cm

**Seeing is Seeing (Part 1)**

2011

oil on canvas

86cm × 71cm

—»

**Before My Time**

2011

oil on linen

72cm × 86cm

129

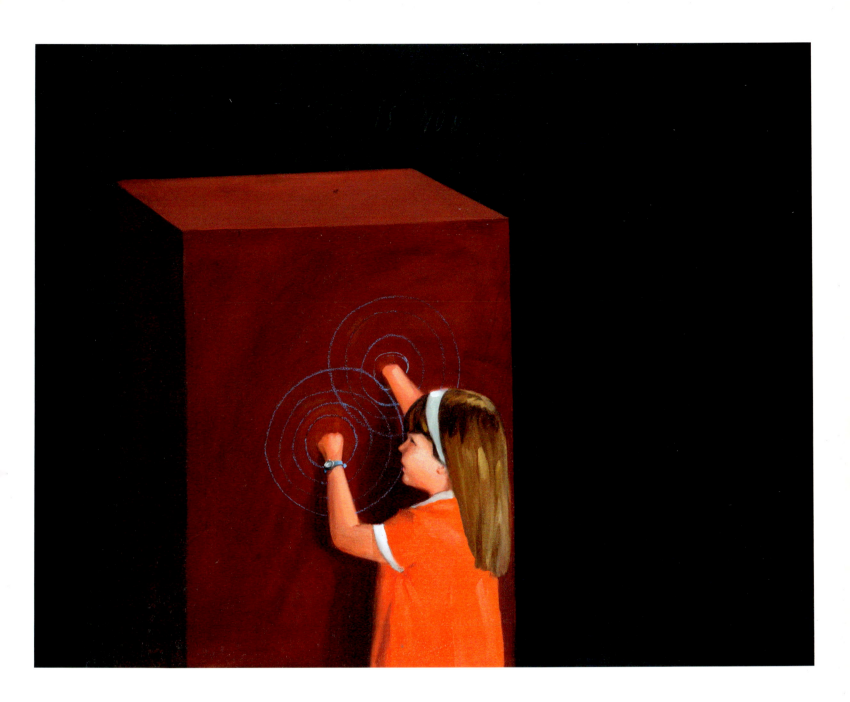

**Out of Reach**
2011
oil and chalk on canvas
71cm × 92cm

«—

**The Jump (Part 1)**
2011
oil and chalk on canvas
115.5cm × 88cm

131

«—

**American Matter (Part 1)**
2010
oil and letraset on canvas
122cm × 92cm

**Portrait with Jesus and Hidden Variables**
2009
acrylic, letraset, and charcoal on salvaged print
65cm × 35cm

In the sciences, hidden variables are used when something occurs that cannot be explained, when a force is at work that is not yet understood. This piece was on display in a New York City restaurant when a member of the public took it down from the wall, removed from its frame, and tore it in half. The top half was never seen again.

133

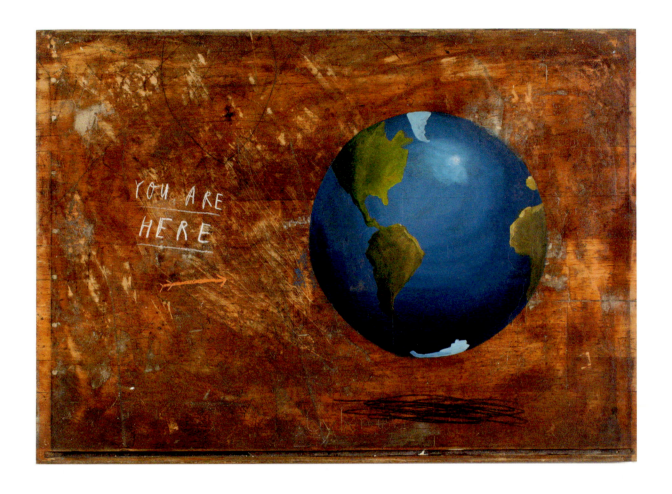

**You are Here**

2011

oil on table top

95cm × 66cm

—»

**New Britannia**

2012

oil on red pine

210cm × 150cm

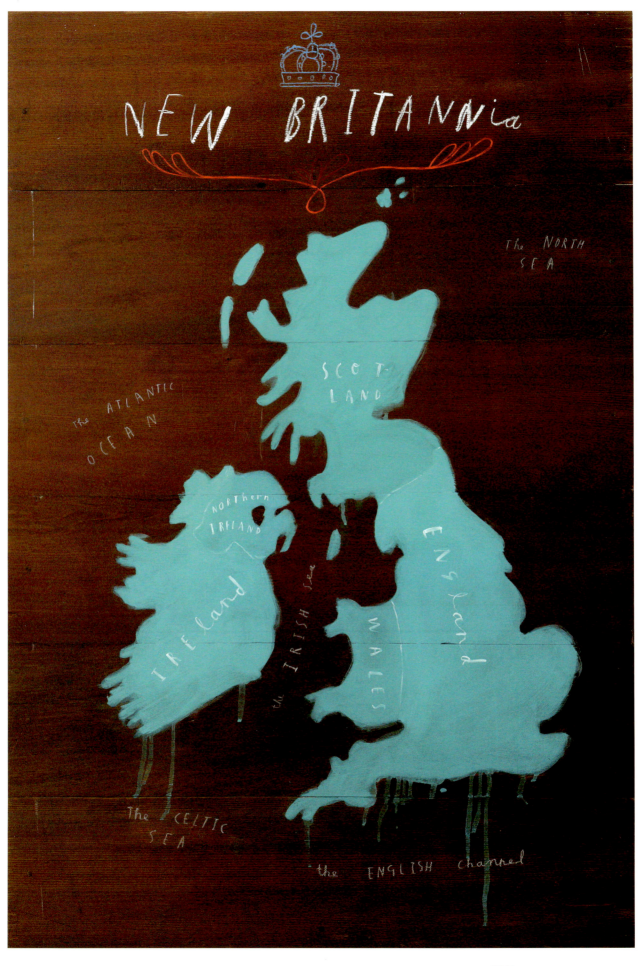

**I Have Trouble Remembering Names (Part 1)**

2012

oil and spectacles with beveled glass on canvas

91cm × 61cm

—»

**I Have Trouble Remembering Names (Part 2)**

2012

oil and spectacles with beveled glass on canvas

91cm × 61cm

**Lost at Lake**

2012

oil on found landscape

71cm × 102cm

**Tragedy at Dawn**

2012

oil on found landscape

74cm × 105cm

—»

**A Point of Light in the Dark**

2012

oil on found landscape

71cm × 132cm

**The Last Request**

2012

paint and collage on found print

83cm × 150cm

**Saturday Morning by the Pool**

2011

oil and enamel on canvas

182cm × 121cm

**Friday Afternoon**
**South Williamsburg**
2011
oil on canvas
183cm × 122cm

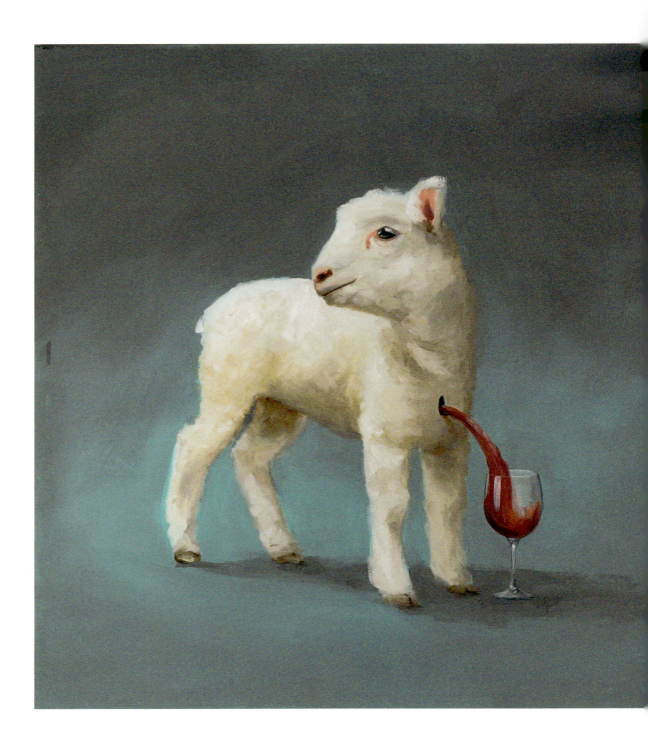

**Decanting and Corking the Lamb of God**

2012

oil on canvas

91cm × 182cm (diptych)

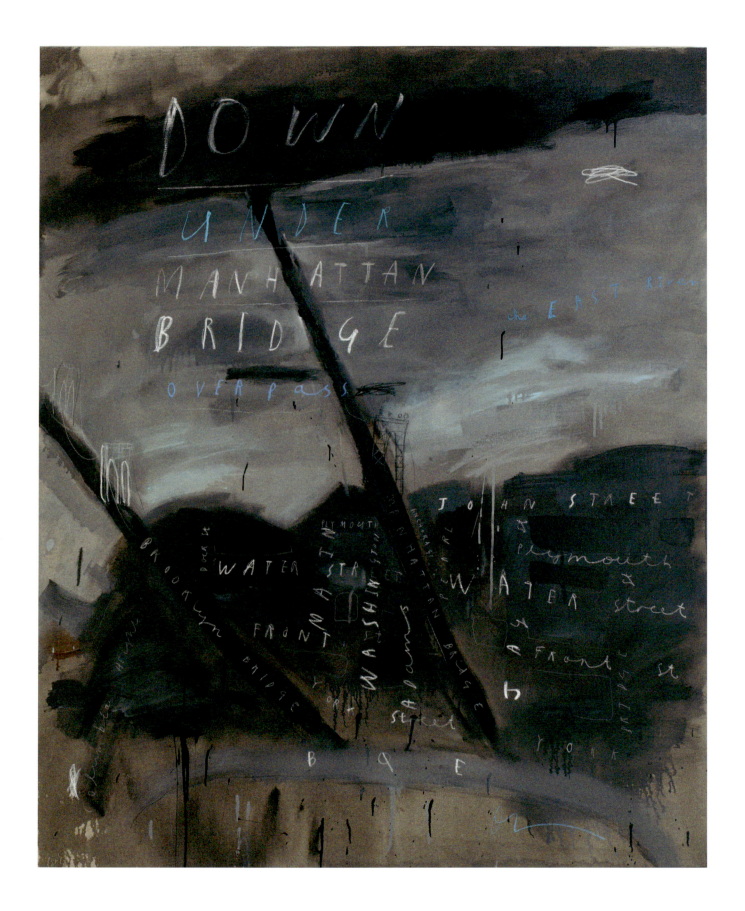

NEW YORK'S DROWNING

**New York's Drowning**

2012

paint and collage on found print

41cm × 63.5cm

**Dumbo**

2012

oil and chalk on canvas

179cm × 147cm

**The Jump (Part 2)**

2012

oil on canvas

102cm × 152cm

**A Song of Innocence and Violence**

2012

mixed media on projection screen

66.5cm × 80cm

**Self Portrait on Mirror**

2012

oil on mirrored glass

51cm × 117cm

**The Wall**

2012

oil on canvas

102cm × 152cm

**Without a Doubt (Part 1)**
2012
oil on canvas in frame dipped in enamel
51cm × 41cm

**Without a Doubt (Part 2)**

2012

oil on canvas in frame dipped in enamel

71cm × 56cm

**Thanks**
Connie Bree
Richard Seabrooke
Conor Nolan
David Wall
Suzanne Mulholland
Elisabeth Honerla
Mac Premo
Adrianna Dufay
Devin Gordon
John Midgley
Kacy Jahanbini
Jeff Burke
Aaron Ruff
Rory Jeffers
Paul Jeffers
Brian Jeffers
Peter Jeffers
Bren Byrne
Charlotte Barker
Dannielle O'Connell
Cate McLaughlin
Dan Leonard
Esther Hwang
Duke Riley
Kitty Joe Sainte-Marie
Gabe Benzur
Lucien Zayan
Simon Courchel
JR
Prune Nourry
Bertrand Delacroix
James Crawford
Malcolm Brown
Chris Heaney
Yng-Ru Chen
Domenica Dunlap
Doreen and Regis
Dr Hugh Morrison
Peter Treiber

**Photography**
John Midgley
Kacy Jahanbini
Malcolm Brown
Christopher Heaney
Mac Premo
David Pauley

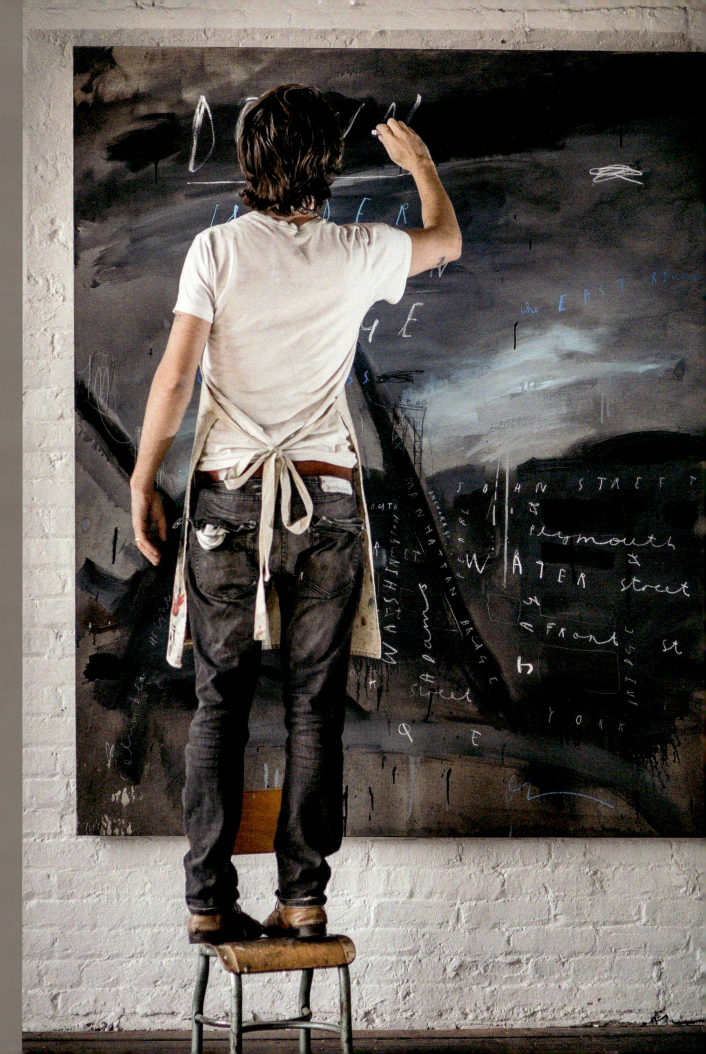

IF YOUR ♥ IS NOT IN AMERICA
YOU HAD
BETTER
GET YOUR OUT

GLUE / LARGE / WATER / SMALL / WEDGE / GOOD
COLOUR